Ni

MW01484203

Quotes & Facts

By Blago Kirov

First Edition

*****

Nikola Tesla: Quotes & Facts
*****

Copyright © 2015 by Blago Kirov

Foreword

Let the future tell the truth and evaluate each one according to his work and accomplishments. The present is theirs; the future, for which I really worked, is mine.

This book is an anthology of quotes from Nikola Tesla and selected facts about Nikola Tesla.

Nikola Tesla was born around midnight, between July 9 and July 10, 1856 during a fierce lightning storm. Tesla was 6 ft 2 in (1.88 m) tall and weighed 142 pounds (64 kg), with almost no weight variance from 1888 to about 1926.
Tesla's eyes were gray-blue.
Nikola Tesla was fluent in many languages besides his native Serbian; he also spoke English, French, German, Italian, Czech, Hungarian and Latin.
Nikola Tesla was good friends with Mark Twain.
Tesla's father Milutin was a Serbian Orthodox priest.
Before entering a building Nikola Tesla would circle the block 3 times.
Tesla had a terrific sense of humor.
Nikola Tesla invented the radio before Guglielmo Marconi, who would receive the Nobel Prize for it.
Nikola Tesla lived many years in New York City, and spent his last decade living there in the Hotel New Yorker. He lived in room 3327, a two-room suite on the 33rd floor.
On January 7, 1943: Nikola Tesla died penniless and alone in room #3327 of the Hotel New Yorker.
After learning of Tesla's death, the FBI ordered the Alien Property Custodian to seize all of Tesla's belongings.

It seems that I have always been ahead of my time. I had to wait nineteen years before Niagara was harnessed by my system, fifteen years before the basic inventions for wireless which I gave to the world in 1893 were applied universally.

Money does not represent such a value as men have placed upon it. All my money has been invested into experiments with which I have made new discoveries enabling mankind to have a little easier life.

Archimedes was my ideal. I admired the works of artists, but to my mind, they were only shadows and semblances. The inventor, I thought, gives to the world creations which are palpable, which live and work.

I have harnessed the cosmic rays and caused them to operate a motive device.

The feeling is constantly growing on me that I had been the first to hear the greeting of one planet to another.

Some Facts about Nikola Tesla

Nikola Tesla was born an ethnic Serb in the village Smiljan, Lika county, in the Austrian Empire (present day Croatia), on 10 July [O.S. 28 June] 1856.

His father, Milutin Tesla (1819–1879), was an Eastern Orthodox priest.

Tesla's mother, Đuka Tesla (née Mandić; 1822–1892), whose father was also an Orthodox priest, had a talent for making home craft tools and mechanical appliances and the ability to memorize Serbian epic poems. Đuka had never received a formal education. Tesla credited his eidetic memory and creative abilities to his mother's genetics and influence.

Tesla's progenitors were from western Serbia, near Montenegro.

Tesla was the fourth of five children. He had three sisters, Milka, Angelina and Marica, and an older brother named Dane, who was killed in a horse riding accident when Tesla was aged five.

In 1861, Tesla attended primary school in Smiljan where he studied German, arithmetic, and religion.

In 1862, the Tesla family moved to the nearby Gospić, Lika where Tesla's father worked as parish priest. Nikola completed primary school, followed by middle school.

In 1870, Tesla moved far north to Karlovac to attend high school at the Higher Real Gymnasium. The classes were held in German, as it was a school within the Austro-Hungarian Military Frontier. Tesla would later write that he became interested in demonstrations of electricity by his physics professor. Tesla noted that these demonstrations of this "mysterious phenomena" made him want "to know more of this wonderful force".

Tesla was able to perform integral calculus in his head, which prompted his teachers to believe that he was cheating. He finished a four-year term in three years, graduating in 1873.

In 1873, Tesla returned to Smiljan. Shortly after he arrived, he contracted cholera, was bedridden for nine months and was near death multiple times. Tesla's father, in a moment of despair, (who had originally wanted him to enter the priesthood) promised to send him to the best engineering school if he recovered from the illness.

In 1874, Tesla evaded conscription into the Austro-Hungarian Army in Smiljan by running away southeast of Lika to Tomingaj, near Gračac. There he explored the mountains wearing hunter's garb. Tesla said that this contact with nature made him stronger, both physically and mentally. He read many books while in Tomingaj and later said that Mark Twain's works had helped him to miraculously recover from his earlier illness.

In 1875, Tesla enrolled at Austrian Polytechnic in Graz, Austria, on a Military Frontier scholarship. During his first year, Tesla never missed a lecture, earned the highest grades possible, passed nine exams (nearly twice as many as required, started a Serb cultural club, and even received a letter of commendation from the dean of the technical faculty to his father, which stated, "Your son is a star of first rank."

During his second year at Austrian Polytechnic in Graz, Tesla came into conflict with Professor Poeschl over the Gramme dynamo, when Tesla suggested that commutators were not necessary.

After his father's death in 1879,Tesla found a package of letters from his professors to his father, warning that unless he were removed from the school, Tesla would die through overwork. Tesla claimed that he worked from 3 a.m. to 11 p.m., no Sundays or holidays excepted. He was "mortified when his father made light of those hard won honors."

At the end of his second year at Austrian Polytechnic in Graz, Tesla lost his scholarship and became addicted to gambling. During his third year, Tesla gambled away his allowance and his tuition money, later gambling back his initial losses and returning the balance to his family. Tesla said that he "conquered his passion then and there," but later in the U.S. he was again known to play billiards.

When examination time came, Tesla was unprepared and asked for an extension to study, but was denied. He did not receive grades for the last semester of the third year and he never graduated from the university.

In December 1878, Tesla left Graz and severed all relations with his family to hide the fact that he dropped out of school. His friends thought that he had drowned in the nearby Mur River. Tesla moved to Maribor, where he worked as a draftsman for 60 florins per month. He spent his spare time playing cards with local men on the streets.

In March 1879, Tesla's father went to Maribor to beg his son to return home, but he refused. Nikola suffered a nervous breakdown around the same time. On 24 March 1879, Tesla was returned to Gospić under police guard for not having a residence permit.

In January 1880, two of Tesla's uncles put together enough money to help him leave Gospić for Prague, where he was to study. He arrived too late to enrol at Charles-Ferdinand University; he had never studied Greek, a required subject; and he was illiterate in Czech, another required subject. Tesla did, however, attend lectures in philosophy at the university as an auditor and he did not receive grades for the courses.

In 1881, Tesla moved to Budapest, Hungary, to work under Tivadar Puskás at a telegraph company, the Budapest Telephone Exchange. Upon arrival, Tesla realized that the company, then under construction, was not functional, so he worked as a draftsman in the Central Telegraph Office instead. Within a few months, the Budapest Telephone Exchange became functional, and Tesla was allocated the chief electrician position. During his employment, Tesla made many improvements to the Central Station equipment and claimed to have perfected a telephone repeater or amplifier, which was never patented nor publicly described.

In 1882, Tivadar Puskás got Tesla another job in Paris with the Continental Edison Company. Tesla began working in what was then a brand new industry, installing indoor incandescent lighting citywide in the form of an electric power utility. The company had several subdivisions and Tesla worked at the Société Electrique Edison, the division in the Ivry-sur-Seine suburb of Paris in charge of installing the lighting system.

There he gained a great deal of practical experience in electrical engineering. Management took of Société Electrique Edison notice of his advanced knowledge in engineering and physics and soon had him designing and building improved versions of generating dynamos and motors. They also sent him on to troubleshoot engineering problems at other Edison utilities being built around France and in Germany.

In 1884, Edison manager Charles Batchelor, who had been overseeing the Paris installation, was brought back to the US to manage the Edison Machine Works, a manufacturing division situated in New York City, and asked that Tesla be brought to the US as well.

In June 1884, Tesla immigrated to the United States.[43] He began working almost immediately at the Machine Works on Manhattan's Lower East Side, an overcrowded shop with a workforce of several hundred machinists, labourers, managing staff, and 20 "field engineers" struggling with the task of building the large electric utility in that city. As in Paris, Tesla was working on troubleshooting installations and improving generators.

Tesla may have met company founder Thomas Alva Edison only a couple of times. One of those times was noted in Tesla's autobiography where, after staying up all night repairing the damaged dynamos on the ocean liner SS Oregon, he ran into Batchelor and Edison, who made a quip about their "Parisian" being out all night. After Tesla told them he had been up all night fixing the Oregon Edison commented to Batchelor that "this is a damned good man."

One of the projects given to Tesla was to develop an arc lamp-based street lighting system. Arc lighting was the most popular type of street lighting but it required high voltages and was incompatible with the Edison low-voltage incandescent system, causing the company to lose contracts in cities that wanted street lighting as well. Tesla's designs were never put into production, possibly because of technical improvements in incandescent street lighting or because of an installation deal that Edison cut with an arc lighting company.

Tesla had been working at the Machine Works for a total of six months when he quit. In his own biography, Tesla stated the manager of the Edison Machine Works offered a $50,000 bonus to design "twenty-four different types of standard machines" "but it turned out to be a practical joke".

The size of the bonus in either story has been noted as odd since Machine Works manager Batchelor was stingy with pay and the company did not have that amount of cash (equivalent to $12 million today) on hand. Tesla's diary contains just one comment on what happened at the end of his employment, a note he scrawled across the two pages covering December 7, 1884, to January 4, 1885, saying "Good by to the Edison Machine Works".

Later versions of this story have Thomas Edison himself offering and then reneging on the deal, quipping "Tesla, you don't understand our American humor."

Soon after leaving the Edison Company Tesla was working on patenting an arc lighting system, possibly the same one he had developed at Edison. In March 1885, he met with patent attorney Lemuel W. Serrell, the same attorney used by Edison, to obtain help with submitting the patents. Serrell introduced Tesla to two businessmen, Robert Lane and Benjamin Vail, who agreed to finance an arc lighting manufacturing and utility company in Tesla's name, the Tesla Electric Light & Manufacturing. Tesla worked for the rest of the year obtaining the patents that included an improved DC generator, the first patents issued to Tesla in the US, and building and installing the system in Rahway, New Jersey Tesla's new system gained notice in the technical press, which commented on its advanced features.

The investors showed little interest in Tesla's ideas for new types of alternating current motors and electrical transmission equipment. After the utility was up and running in 1886, they decided that the manufacturing side of the business was too competitive and opted to simply run an electric utility. They formed a new utility company, abandoning Tesla's company and leaving the inventor penniless. Tesla even lost control of the patents he had generated, since he had assigned them to the company in exchange for stock.

He had to work at various electrical repair jobs and as a ditch digger for $2 per day. Later in life Tesla would recount that part of 1886 as a time of hardship, writing "My high education in various branches of science, mechanics and literature seemed to me like a mockery".

In late 1886, Tesla met Alfred S. Brown, a Western Union superintendent, and New York attorney Charles F. Peck. The two men were experienced in setting up companies and promoting inventions and patents for financial gain. Based on Tesla's new ideas for electrical equipment, including a thermo-magnetic motor idea, they agreed to back the inventor financially and handle his patents. Together they formed the Tesla Electric Company in April 1887, with an agreement that profits from generated patents would go 1/3 to Tesla, 1/3 to Peck and Brown, and 1/3 to fund development. They set up a laboratory for Tesla at 89 Liberty Street in Manhattan, where he worked on improving and developing new types of electric motors, generators, and other devices.

In 1887, Tesla developed an induction motor that ran on alternating current (AC), a power system format that was rapidly expanding in Europe and the United States because of its advantages in long-distance, high-voltage transmission. The motor used polyphase current, which generated a rotating magnetic field to turn the motor (a principle that Tesla claimed to have conceived in 1882). This innovative electric motor, patented in May 1888, was a simple self-starting design that did not need a commutator, thus avoiding sparking and the high maintenance of constantly servicing and replacing mechanical brushes.

Along with getting the motor patented, Peck and Brown arranged to get the motor publicized, starting with independent testing to verify it was a functional improvement, followed by press releases sent to technical publications for articles to run concurrent with the issue of the patent. Physicist William Arnold Anthony (who tested the motor) and Electrical World magazine editor Thomas Commerford Martin arranged for Tesla to demonstrate his AC motor on 16 May 1888 at the American Institute of Electrical Engineers.

During 1888, Tesla worked in Pittsburgh, helping to create an alternating current system to power the city's streetcars. He found it a frustrating period because of conflicts with the other Westinghouse engineers over how best to implement AC power.

Tesla's demonstration of his induction motor and Westinghouse's subsequent licensing of the patent, both in 1888, came at the time of extreme competition between electric companies. The three big firms, Westinghouse, Edison, and Thompson-Houston, were trying to grow in a capital-intensive business while financially undercutting each other. There was even a "War of Currents" propaganda campaign going on with Edison Electric trying to claim their direct current system was better and safer than the Westinghouse alternating current system. Competing in this market meant Westinghouse would not have the cash or engineering resources to develop Tesla's motor and the related polyphase system right away.

Tesla agreed to release the company from the royalty payment clause in the contract. Six years later Westinghouse would purchase Tesla's patent for a lump sum payment of $216,000 as part of a patent-sharing agreement signed with General Electric (a company created from the 1892 merger of Edison and Thompson-Houston).

The money Tesla made from licensing his AC patents made him independently wealthy and gave him the time and funds to pursue his own interests. In 1889, Tesla moved out of the Liberty Street shop Peck and Brown had rented and for the next dozen years would work out of a series of workshop/laboratory spaces in Manhattan. These included a lab at 175 Grand Street (1889–1892), the fourth floor of 33–35 South Fifth Avenue (1892–1895), and sixth and seventh floors of 46 & 48 East Houston Street (1895–1902). Tesla and his hired staff would conduct some of his most significant work in these workshops.

In the summer of 1889, Tesla traveled to the 1889 Exposition Universelle in Paris and learned of Heinrich Hertz' 1886–88 experiments that proved the existence of electromagnetic radiation, including radio waves. Tesla tried powering a Ruhmkorff coil with a high speed alternator he had been developing as part of an improved arc lighting system but found that the high frequency current overheated the iron core and melted the insulation between the primary and secondary windings in the coil. To fix this problem Tesla came up with his Tesla coil with an air gap instead of insulating material between the primary and secondary windings and an iron core that could be moved to different positions in or out of the coil.

On 30 July 1891, aged 35, Tesla became a naturalized citizen of the United States. In the same year, he patented his Tesla coil.

After 1890, Tesla experimented with transmitting power by inductive and capacitive coupling using high AC voltages generated with his Tesla coil. He attempted to develop a wireless lighting system based on near-field inductive and capacitive coupling and conducted a series of public demonstrations where he lit Geissler tubes and even incandescent light bulbs from across a stage. He would spend most of the decade working on variations of this new form of lighting with the help of various investors but none of the ventures succeeded in making a commercial product out of his findings.

In 1893 at St. Louis, Missouri, the Franklin Institute in Philadelphia, Pennsylvania and the National Electric Light Association, Tesla told onlookers that he was sure a system like his could eventually conduct "intelligible signals or perhaps even power to any distance without the use of wires" by conducting it through the Earth.

Tesla served as a vice-president of the American Institute of Electrical Engineers from 1892 to 1894, the forerunner of the modern-day IEEE (along with the Institute of Radio Engineers).

Trying to come up with a better way to generate alternating current, Tesla developed a steam powered reciprocating electricity generator. He patented it in 1893 and introduced it at the Chicago World's Columbian Exposition that year. Steam would be forced into the oscillator and rush out through a series of ports, pushing a piston up and down that was attached to an armature. The magnetic armature vibrated up and down at high speed, producing an alternating magnetic field. This induced alternating electric current in the wire coils located adjacent. It did away with the complicated parts of a steam engine/generator, but never caught on as a feasible engineering solution to generate electricity.

In 1893-94 Tesla showed a series of electrical effects related to alternating current as well as his wireless lighting system, using a demonstration he had previously performed throughout America and Europe; these included using high-voltage, high-frequency alternating current to light a wireless gas-discharge lamp. Tesla also explained the principles of the rotating magnetic field in an induction motor by demonstrating how to make a copper egg stand on end, using a device that he constructed known as the Egg of Columbus and introduced his new steam powered oscillator AC generator.

In 1893, Edward Dean Adams, who headed up the Niagara Falls Cataract Construction Company, sought Tesla's opinion on what system would be best to transmit power generated at the falls. Tesla advised Adams that a two-phased system would be the most reliable, and that there was a Westinghouse system to light incandescent bulbs using two-phase alternating current. The company awarded a contract to Westinghouse Electric for building a two-phase AC generating system at the Niagara Falls, based on Tesla's advice and Westinghouse's demonstration at the Columbian Exposition that they could build a complete AC system. At the same time, a further contract was awarded to General Electric to build the AC distribution system.

In 1895, Edward Dean Adams, impressed with what he saw when he toured Tesla's lab, agreed to help found the Nikola Tesla Company, set up to fund, develop, and market a variety of previous Tesla patents and inventions as well as new ones. Alfred Brown signed on, bringing along patents developed under Peck and Brown. The board was filled out with William Birch Rankine and Charles F. Coaney. It found few investors; the mid-1890s was a tough time financially, and the wireless lighting and oscillators patents it was set up to market never panned out. The company would handle Tesla's patents for decades to come.

In the early morning hours of March 13, 1895, the South Fifth Avenue building that housed Tesla's lab caught fire. It started in the basement of the building and was so intense Tesla's 4th floor lab burned and collapsed into the second floor. The fire not only set back Tesla's ongoing projects, it destroyed a collection of early notes and research material, models, and demonstration pieces, including many that had been exhibited at the 1893 Worlds Colombian Exposition. Tesla told The New York Times "I am in too much grief to talk. What can I say?" After the fire Tesla moved to 46 & 48 East Houston Street and rebuilt his lab on the 6th and 7th floors.

In March 1896, after hearing of Wilhelm Röntgen's discovery of X-ray and X-ray imaging (radiography), Tesla proceeded to do his own experiments in X-ray imaging, developing a high energy single terminal vacuum tube of his own design that had no target electrode and that worked from the output of the Tesla Coil (the modern term for the phenomenon produced by this device is bremsstrahlung or braking radiation). In his research, Tesla devised several experimental setups to produce X-rays.

In 1898, Tesla demonstrated a boat that used a coherer-based radio control—which he dubbed "telautomaton"—to the public during an electrical exhibition at Madison Square Garden. The crowd that witnessed the demonstration made outrageous claims about the workings of the boat, such as magic, telepathy, and being piloted by a trained monkey hidden inside. Tesla tried to sell his idea to the U.S. military as a type of radio-controlled torpedo, but they showed little interest. Remote radio control remained a novelty until World War I.

From the 1890s through 1906, Tesla spent a great deal of his time and fortune on a series of projects trying to develop the transmission of electrical power without wires. It was an expansion of his idea of using coils to transmit power that he had been demonstrating in wireless lighting. He saw this as not only a way to transmit large amounts of power around the world but also, as he had pointed out in his earlier lectures, a way to transmit worldwide communications.

By the mid 1890s, Tesla was working on the idea that he might be able to conduct electricity long distance through the Earth or the atmosphere, and began working on experiments to test this idea including setting up a large resonance transformer magnifying transmitter in his East Houston Street lab. Seeming to borrow from a common idea at the time that the Earth's atmosphere was conductive, he proposed a system composed of balloons suspending, transmitting, and receiving, electrodes in the air above 30,000 feet (9,100 m) in altitude, where he thought the lower pressure would allow him to send high voltages (millions of volts) long distances.

To further study the conductive nature of low pressure air, Tesla set up an experimental station at high altitude in Colorado Springs during 1899. There he could safely operate much larger coils than in the cramped confines of his New York lab, and an associate had made an arrangement for the El Paso Power Company to supply alternating current free of charge. There he conducted experiments with a large coil operating in the megavolts range, producing artificial lightning (and thunder) consisting of millions of volts and up to 135 feet (41 m) long discharges and, at one point, inadvertently burned out the generator in El Paso, causing a power outage.

During his time at his laboratory, Tesla observed unusual signals from his receiver which he speculated to be communications from another planet. He mentioned them in a letter to a reporter in December 1899 and to the Red Cross Society in December 1900. Reporters treated it as a sensational story and jumped to the conclusion Tesla was hearing signals from Mars.[151] He expanded on the signals he heard in a 9 February 1901 Collier's Weekly article "Talking With Planets" where he said it had not been immediately apparent to him that he was hearing "intelligently controlled signals" and that the signals could come from Mars, Venus, or other planets.

In March 1901, he obtained $150,000 ($4,412,400 in today's dollars from J. Pierpont Morgan in return for a 51% share of any generated wireless patents, and began planning the Wardenclyffe Tower facility to be built in Shoreham, New York, 100 miles (161 km) east of the city on the North Shore of Long Island.

By July 1901, Tesla had expanded his plans to build a more powerful transmitter to leap ahead of Marconi's radio based system, which Tesla thought was a copy of his own system. He approached Morgan to ask for more money to build the larger system but Morgan refused to supply any further funds.

A month after Marconi's success, Tesla tried to get Morgan to back an even larger plan to transmit messages and power by controlling "vibrations throughout the globe". Over the next five years, Tesla wrote more than 50 letters to Morgan, pleading for and demanding additional funding to complete the construction of Wardenclyffe. Tesla continued the project for another nine months into 1902. The tower was erected to its full 187 feet (57 m). In June 1902, Tesla moved his lab operations from Houston Street to Wardenclyffe.

Investors on Wall Street were putting their money into Marconi's system, and some in the press began turning against Tesla's project, claiming it was a hoax. The project came to a halt in 1905, and in 1906, the financial problems and other events may have led a nervous breakdown on Tesla's part. Tesla mortgaged the Wardenclyffe property to cover his debts at the Waldorf-Astoria. He lost the property in foreclosure in 1915, and in 1917 the Tower was demolished by the new owner to make the land a more viable real estate asset.

After Wardencyiffe closed, Tesla continued to write to Morgan; after his died, Tesla wrote to his son Jack Morgan, trying to get further funding for the project. In 1906, Tesla opened offices at 165 Broadway in Manhattan, trying to raise further funds by developing and marketing his patents. He went on to have offices at the Metropolitan Life Tower from 1910 to 1914; rented for a few months at the Woolworth Building, moving out because he could not afford the rent; and then to office space at 8 West 40th Street from 1915 to 1925. After moving to 8 West 40th Street, he was effectively bankrupt. Most of his patents had run out and he was having trouble with the new inventions he was trying to develop.

Since 1900, Tesla had been living at the Waldorf Astoria in New York running up a large bill. In 1922, he moved to St. Regis Hotel and would follow a pattern from then on of moving to a new hotel every few years leaving behind unpaid bills.

Tesla would walk to the park every day to feed the pigeons. He took to feeding them at the window of his hotel room and bringing the injured ones in to nurse back to health. He said that he had been visited by a specific injured white pigeon daily. Tesla spent over $2,000, including building a device that comfortably supported her so her bones could heal, to fix her broken wing and leg.

Tesla's unpaid bills, and complaints about the mess from his pigeon-feeding, forced him to leave the St. Regis in 1923, the Hotel Pennsylvania in 1930, and the Hotel Governor Clinton in 1934. At one point, he also took rooms at the Hotel Marguery.

In 1934, Tesla moved to the Hotel New Yorker, and Westinghouse Electric & Manufacturing Company began paying him $125 per month as well as paying his rent, expenses the Company would pay for the rest of Tesla's life.

In 1931, Kenneth Swezey, a young writer who had been associated with Tesla for some time, organized a celebration for the inventor's 75th birthday. Tesla received congratulatory letters from more than 70 pioneers in science and engineering, including Albert Einstein, and he was also featured on the cover of Time magazine.

At the 1932 occasion, Tesla claimed he had invented a motor that would run on cosmic rays.

In 1933, at age 77, Tesla told reporters that, after thirty-five years of work, he was on the verge of producing proof of a new form of energy. He claimed it was a theory of energy that was "violently opposed" to Einsteinian physics, and could be tapped with an apparatus that would be cheap to run and last 500 years. He also told reporters he was working on a way to transmit individualized private radio wavelengths, working on breakthroughs in metallurgy, and developing a way to photograph the retina to record thought.

At the 1934 party, Tesla told reporters he had designed a superweapon he claimed would end all war. He would call it "teleforce", but was usually referred to as his death ray. Tesla described it as a defensive weapon that would be put up along the border of a country to be used against attacking ground-based infantry or aircraft. Tesla never revealed detailed plans of how the weapon worked during his lifetime, but in 1984, they surfaced at the Nikola Tesla Museum archive in Belgrade. The treatise, The New Art of Projecting Concentrated Non-dispersive Energy through the Natural Media, described an open-ended vacuum tube with a gas jet seal that allows particles to exit, a method of charging slugs of tungsten or mercury to millions of volts, and directing them in streams (through electrostatic repulsion). Tesla tried to interest the US War Department, the United Kingdom, the Soviet Union, and Yugoslavia in the device.

In 1935, at his 79th birthday party, Tesla covered many topics. He claimed to have discovered the cosmic ray in 1896 and invented a way to produce direct current by induction, and made many claims about his mechanical oscillator. Describing the device (which he expected would earn him $100 million within two years) he told reporters that a version of his oscillator had caused an earthquake in his 46 East Houston Street lab and neighboring streets in downtown New York City in 1898. He went on to tell reporters his oscillator could destroy the Empire State Building with 5 lbs of air pressure. He also explained a new technique he developed using his oscillators he called "Telegeodynamics", using it to transmit vibrations into the ground that he claimed would work over any distance to be used for communication or locating underground mineral deposits.

At his 1937 celebration in the Grand Ballroom of Hotel New Yorker, Tesla received the "Order of the White Lion" from the Czechoslovakia ambassador and a medal from the Yugoslavian ambassador. On questions concerning the death ray, Tesla stated, "But it is not an experiment ... I have built, demonstrated and used it. Only a little time will pass before I can give it to the world."

In the fall of 1937, after midnight one night, Tesla left the Hotel New Yorker to make his regular commute to the cathedral and the library to feed the pigeons. While crossing a street a couple of blocks from the hotel, Tesla was unable to dodge a moving taxicab and was thrown to the ground. His back was severely wrenched and three of his ribs were broken in the accident. The full extents of his injuries were never known; Tesla refused to consult a doctor, an almost lifelong custom, and never fully recovered.

Tesla died alone in Room 3327 of the New Yorker Hotel on 7 January 1943, at the age of 86. His body was later found by maid Alice Monaghan after she had entered Tesla's room, ignoring the "do not disturb" sign that Tesla had placed on his door two days earlier. Assistant medical examiner H.W. Wembley examined the body and ruled that the cause of death had been coronary thrombosis.

Two days after his death the Federal Bureau of Investigation ordered the Alien Property Custodian to seize Tesla's belongings, even though Tesla was an American citizen. John G. Trump, a professor at M.I.T. and a well-known electrical engineer serving as a technical aide to the National Defense Research Committee, was called in to analyze the Tesla items, which were being held in custody. After a three-day investigation, Trump's report concluded that there was nothing which would constitute a hazard in unfriendly hands.

In a box purported to contain a part of Tesla's "death ray", Trump found a 45-year-old multidecade resistance box.

Some of Tesla's patents are not accounted for, and various sources have discovered some that have lain hidden in patent archives. There are a minimum of 278 known patents issued to Tesla in 26 countries. Many of Tesla's patents were in the United States, Britain, and Canada, but many other patents were approved in countries around the globe. Many inventions developed by Tesla were not put into patent protection.

Tesla worked every day from 9:00 a.m. until 6:00 p.m. or later, with dinner from exactly 8:10 p.m., at Delmonico's restaurant and later the Waldorf-Astoria Hotel. Tesla would telephone his dinner order to the headwaiter, who also could be the only one to serve him. The meal was required to be ready at eight o'clock ... He dined alone, except on the rare occasions when he would give a dinner to a group to meet his social obligations. Tesla would then resume his work, often until 3:00 a.m.

For exercise, Tesla walked between 8 and 10 miles (13 and 16 km) per day.

He curled his toes one hundred times for each foot every night, saying that it stimulated his brain cells.

In an interview with newspaper editor Arthur Brisbane, Tesla said that he did not believe in telepathy, stating, "Suppose I made up my mind to murder you," he said, "In a second you would know it. Now, isn't that wonderful? By what process does the mind get at all this?" In the same interview, Tesla said that he believed that all fundamental laws could be reduced to one.

Tesla became a vegetarian in his later years, living on only milk, bread, honey, and vegetable juices.

Tesla was 6 feet 2 inches (1.88 m) tall and weighed 142 pounds (64 kg), with almost no weight variance from 1888 to about 1926. His appearance was described by newspaper editor Arthur Brisbane as "almost the tallest, almost the thinnest and certainly the most serious man who goes to Delmonico's regularly". He was an elegant, stylish figure in New York City, meticulous in his grooming, clothing, and regimented in his daily activities, an appearance he maintained as to further his business relationships. He was also described as having light eyes, "very big hands", and "remarkably big" thumbs.

Tesla read many works, memorizing complete books, and supposedly possessed a photographic memory.

He was a polyglot, speaking eight languages: Serbo-Croatian, Czech, English, French, German, Hungarian, Italian, and Latin.

Tesla related in his autobiography that he experienced detailed moments of inspiration. He suffered a peculiar affliction in which blinding flashes of light would appear before his eyes, often accompanied by visions. Often, the visions were linked to a word or idea he might have come across; at other times they would provide the solution to a particular problem he had encountered. Just by hearing the name of an item, he would be able to envision it in realistic detail.

Tesla would visualize an invention in his mind with extreme precision, including all dimensions, before moving to the construction stage, a technique sometimes known as picture thinking. He typically did not make drawings by hand but worked from memory.

Beginning in his childhood, Tesla had frequent flashbacks to events that had happened previously in his life.

Tesla claimed never to sleep more than two hours per night.

On one occasion at his laboratory, Tesla worked for a period of 84 hours without rest.

Tesla never married, explaining that his chastity was very helpful to his scientific abilities.

He once said in earlier years that he felt he could never be worthy enough for a woman, considering women superior in every way.

Tesla was a good friend of Francis Marion Crawford, Robert Underwood Johnson, Stanford White, Fritz Lowenstein, George Scherff, and Kenneth Swezey.

In middle age, Tesla became a close friend of Mark Twain; they spent a lot of time together in his lab and elsewhere. Twain notably described Tesla's induction motor invention as "the most valuable patent since the telephone."

Tesla could be harsh at times and openly expressed disgust for overweight people, such as when he fired a secretary because of her weight. He was quick to criticize clothing; on several occasions, Tesla directed a subordinate to go home and change her dress.

When Thomas Edison died, in 1931, Tesla contributed the only negative opinion to The New York Times, buried in an extensive coverage of Edison's life: "He had no hobby, cared for no sort of amusement of any kind and lived in utter disregard of the most elementary rules of hygiene ..."

Tesla's image is on the current 100 Serbian dinar banknote.

Belgrade airport was renamed 'Belgrade Nikola Tesla Airport' in honor of Tesla's 150th birthday on July 10, 2006.

The Tesla crater on the far side of the moon and planetoid 2244 Tesla are named in tribute of him.

Nikola Tesla claimed to have devised a "Dynamic theory of gravity" which disagreed with the model of Einstein's General Theory of Relativity; but his theory was never published, and no comprehensive notes are to be found on the subject.

Nikola Tesla was born around midnight, between July 9 and July 10, 1856 during a fierce lightning storm.

Tesla's eyes were gray-blue.

Before entering a building Nikola Tesla would circle the block 3 times.

Tesla had a terrific sense of humour.

The French actress Sarah Bernhardt was very interested in Nikola Tesla but he found her to be a mere distraction. He was obsessed by his work.

There is a bronze statue of Nikola Tesla sitting with a book on his lap in Niagara Falls State Park on Goat Island, New York.

After dining with writer and poet Rudyard Kipling, Nikola Tesla wrote this in a correspondence to a close friend: My dear Mrs. Johnson, What is the matter with ink spiller Kipling? He actually dared to invite me to dine in an obscure hotel where I would be sure to get hair and cockroaches in the soup."

Nikola Tesla worked on inventing machines that ran on renewable resource, such as solar power and hydroelectricity.

Nikola Tesla patented the first speedometer for cars.

Tesla's Obsessive-Compulsive Disorder (OCD), which was not a classified illness in his time but considered a symptom of insanity, made him obsess over the number three where every hotel he stayed at had to include a 3.

Nikola Tesla would always sit at the same table at his hotel restaurants.

Nikola Tesla has always 18 napkins brought over so he can clean his silverware, plates, and glasses due to his great fear of germs.

Nikola Tesla never shook hands with people due to his great fear of germs.

Nikola Tesla was disgusted by anyone else's hair.

Nikola Tesla hated jewelry especially pearl necklaces.

Nikola Tesla loathed perfume.

Nikola Tesla also talked about experiments that suggested particles with fractional charges of an electron. In 1977 they were "discovered" as quarks.

The rock band Tesla is named after Nikola Tesla.

A museum in honor of his work, known as the Nikola Tesla Museum is located in Belgrade, Serbia.

In 1928 Nikola Tesla received his last patent, which was a forerunner to the modern day helicopter.

Orson Wells played Tesla in the 1980 Yugoslavian film "The Secret of Nikola Tesla".

Nikola Tesla worked for many years attempting his wireless transmission of electricity and believed that electricity could be projected into the upper atmosphere for storage and access at will.
Nikola Tesla Museum holds more than 160,000 original documents and works of Tesla, as well as a Urn with Tesla's ashes.

Nikola Tesla believed in eugenics. He seemed to think that some people just weren't fit to produce offspring. He wrote in a 1935 magazine article: "The trend of opinion among eugenics's is that we must make marriage more difficult. Certainly no one who is not a desirable parent should be permitted to produce progeny. A century from now it will no more occur to a normal person to mate with a person eugenically unfit than to marry a habitual criminal."

Tesla believed that atoms are immutable—they could not change state or be split in any way. He was a believer in the 19th century concept of an all-pervasive "ether" that transmitted electrical energy.

Tesla claimed to have developed his own physical principle regarding matter and energy that he started working on in 1892, and in 1937, at age 81, claimed in a letter to have completed a "dynamic theory of gravity" that "[would] put an end to idle speculations and false conceptions, as that of curved space." He stated that the theory was "worked out in all details" and that he hoped to soon give it to the world.

Tesla was raised an Orthodox Christian. Later in life he did not consider himself to be a "believer in the orthodox sense," said he opposed religious fanaticism, and said "Buddhism and Christianity are the greatest religions both in number of disciples and in importance". He also said "To me, the universe is simply a great machine which never came into being and never will end" and "what we call 'soul' or 'spirit,' is nothing more than the sum of the functioning of the body. When this functioning ceases, the 'soul' or the 'spirit' ceases likewise".

His Words

Money does not represent such a value as men have placed upon it· All my money has been invested into experiments with which I have made new discoveries enabling mankind to have a little easier life·

Archimedes was my ideal. I admired the works of artists, but to my mind, they were only shadows and semblances. The inventor, I thought, gives to the world creations which are palpable, which live and work.

I have harnessed the cosmic rays and caused them to operate a motive device.

The feeling is constantly growing on me that I had been the first to hear the greeting of one planet to another.

It seems that I have always been ahead of my time. I had to wait nineteen years before Niagara was harnessed by my system, fifteen years before the basic inventions for wireless which I gave to the world in 1893 were applied universally.

Let the future tell the truth and evaluate each one according to his work and accomplishments. The present is theirs; the future, for which I really worked, is mine.

A state of human life vaguely defined by the term "Universal Peace," while a result of cumulative effort through centuries past, might come into existence quickly, not unlike a crystal suddenly forms in a solution which has been slowly prepared. But just as no effect can precede its cause, so this state can never be brought on by any pact between nations, however solemn. Experience is made before the law is formulated; both are related like cause and effect. So long as we are clearly conscious of the expectation, that peace is to result from such a parliamentary decision, so long have we conclusive evidence that we are not fit for peace. Only then when we shall feel that such international meetings are mere formal procedures, unnecessary except in so far as they might serve to give definite expression to a common desire, will peace be assured.

It seems that I have always been ahead of my time.

According to an adopted theory, every ponderable atom is differentiated from a tenuous fluid, filling all space merely by spinning motion, as a whirl of water in a calm lake. By being set in movement this fluid, the ether, becomes gross matter. Its movement arrested, the primary substance reverts to its normal state. It appears, then, possible for man through harnessed energy of the medium and suitable agencies for starting and stopping ether whirls to cause matter to form and disappear. At his command, almost without effort on his part, old worlds would vanish and new ones would spring into being. He could alter the size of this planet, control its seasons, adjust its distance from the sun, guide it on its eternal journey along any path he might choose, through the depths of the universe. He could make planets collide and produce his suns and stars, his heat and light; he could originate life in all its infinite forms. To cause at will the birth and death of matter would be man's grandest deed, which would give him the mastery of physical creation, make him fulfill his ultimate destiny.

All knowledge or form conception is evoked through the medium of the eye, either in response to disturbances directly received on the retina or to their fainter secondary effects and reverberations. Other sense organs can only call forth feelings which have no reality of existence and of which no conception can be formed.

As in nature, all is ebb and tide, all is wave motion, so it seems that in all branches of industry, alternating currents - electric wave motion - will have the sway.

By an irony of fate, my first employment was as a draughtsman. I hated drawing; it was for me the very worst of annoyances. Fortunately, it was not long before I secured the position I sought, that of chief electrician to the telephone company.

Einstein's relativity work is a magnificent mathematical garb which fascinates dazzles and makes people blind to the underlying errors. The theory is like a beggar clothed in purple whom ignorant people take for a king... its exponents are brilliant men but they are metaphysicists rather than scientists.

Electric current, after passing into the earth travels to the diametrically opposite region of the same and rebounding from there, returns to its point of departure with virtually undiminished force. The outgoing and returning currents clash and form nodes and loops similar to those observable on a vibrating cord. To traverse the entire distance of about twenty-five thousand miles, equal to the circumference of the globe, the current requires a certain time interval, which I have approximately ascertained. In yielding this knowledge, nature has revealed one of its most precious secrets, of inestimable consequence to man. So astounding are the facts in this connection, that it would seem as though the Creator, himself, had electrically designed this planet just for the purpose of enabling us to achieve wonders which, before my discovery, could not have been conceived by the wildest imagination.

The inventor, I thought, gives to the world
creations which are palpable, which live and
work.

Electrical science has revealed to us the true nature of light, has provided us with innumerable appliances and instruments of precision, and has thereby vastly added to the exactness of our knowledge.

Every living being is an engine geared to the wheelwork of the universe. Though seemingly affected only by its immediate surrounding, the sphere of external influence extends to infinite distance.

Fights between individuals, as well as governments and nations, invariably result from misunderstandings in the broadest interpretation of this term. Misunderstandings are always caused by the inability of appreciating one another's point of view. This again is due to the ignorance of those concerned, not so much in their own, as in their mutual fields. The peril of a clash is aggravated by a more or less predominant sense of combativeness, posed by every human being. To resist this inherent fighting tendency the best way is to dispel ignorance of the doings of others by a systematic spread of general knowledge. With this object in view, it is most important to aid exchange of thought and intercourse.

For ages this idea has been proclaimed in the consummately wise teachings of religion, probably not alone as a means of insuring peace and harmony among men, but as a deeply founded truth. The Buddhist expresses it in one way, the Christian in another, but both say the same: We are all one.

From childhood I was compelled to concentrate attention upon myself. This caused me much suffering, but to my present view, it was a blessing in disguise for it has taught me to appreciate the inestimable value of introspection in the preservation of life, as well as a means of achievement.

From my childhood I had been intended for the clergy. This prospect hung like a dark cloud on my mind.

General disarmament being for the present entirely out of question, a proportionate reduction might be recommended. The safety of any country and of the world's commerce depending not on the absolute, but relative amount of war material, this would be evidently the first reasonable step to take towards universal economy and peace. But it would be a hopeless task to establish an equitable basis of adjustment. Population, naval strength, force of army, commercial importance, water-power, or any other natural resource, actual or prospective, are equally unsatisfactory standards to consider.

I am credited with being one of the hardest workers and perhaps I am, if thought is the equivalent of labour, for I have devoted to it almost all of my waking hours. But if work is interpreted to be a definite performance in a specified time according to a rigid rule, then I may be the worst of idlers. Every effort under compulsion demands a sacrifice of life-energy. I never paid such a price. On the contrary, I have thrived on my thoughts.

I constructed a laboratory in the neighborhood of Pike's Peak· The conditions in the pure air of the Colorado Mountains proved extremely favorable for my experiments, and the results were most gratifying to me·

I do not think there is any thrill that can go through the human heart like that felt by the inventor as he sees some creation of the brain unfolding to success ... Such emotions make a man forget food, sleep, friends, love, everything.

I do not think you can name many great inventions that have been made by married men.

I feel convinced that my preservation was not altogether accidental, but was indeed the work of divine power. An inventor's endeavor is essentially life saving. Whether he harnesses forces, improves devices, or provides new comforts and conveniences, he is adding to the safety of our existence. He is also better qualified than the average individual to protect himself in peril, for he is observant and resourceful.

I have already demonstrated, by crucial tests, the practicability of signaling by my system from one to any other point of the globe, no matter how remote, and I shall soon convert the disbelievers.

I have obtained... spark discharges extending through more than one hundred feet and carrying currents of one thousand amperes, electromotive forces approximating twenty million volts, chemically active streamers covering areas of several thousand square feet, and electrical disturbances in the natural media surpassing those caused by lightning, in intensity.

I hold that space cannot be curved, for the simple reason that it can have no properties. It might as well be said that God has properties. He has not, but only attributes and these are of our own making. Of properties we can only speak when dealing with matter filling the space. To say that in the presence of large bodies space becomes curved is equivalent to stating that something can act upon nothing. I, for one, refuse to subscribe to such a view.

I myself eschew all stimulants. I also practically abstain from meat.

If we want to reduce poverty and misery, if we want to give to every deserving individual what is needed for a safe existence of an intelligent being, we want to provide more machinery, more power. Power is our mainstay, the primary source of our many-sided energies.

In a time not distant, it will be possible to flash any image formed in thought on a screen and render it visible at any place desired. The perfection of this means of reading thought will create a revolution for the better in all our social relations.

In the twenty-first century, the robot will take the place which slave labor occupied in ancient civilization.

It is paradoxical, yet true, to say, that the more we know, the more ignorant we become in the absolute sense, for it is only through enlightenment that we become conscious of our limitations. Precisely one of the most gratifying results of intellectual evolution is the continuous opening up of new and greater prospects.

It should be borne in mind that electrical energy obtained by harnessing a waterfall is probably fifty times more effective than fuel energy. Since this is the most perfect way of rendering the sun's energy available, the direction of the future material development of man is clearly indicated.

Man's new sense of pity began to interfere with the ruthless workings of nature. The only method compatible with our notions of civilization and the race is to prevent the breeding of the unfit by sterilization and the deliberate guidance of the mating instinct. The trend of opinion among eugenists is that we must make marriage more difficult. Certainly no one who is not a desirable parent should be permitted to produce progeny. A century from now it will no more occur to a normal person to mate with a person eugenically unfit than to marry a habitual criminal.

Marconi is a good fellow. Let him continue. He is using seventeen of my patents.

Modern science says: 'The sun is the past, the earth is the present, the moon is the future.' From an incandescent mass we have originated, and into a frozen mass we shall turn. Merciless is the law of nature, and rapidly and irresistibly we are drawn to our doom.

Most persons are so absorbed in the contemplation of the outside world that they are wholly oblivious to what is passing on within themselves. The premature death of millions is primarily traceable to this cause. Even among those who exercise care, it is a common mistake to avoid imaginary, and ignore the real dangers. And what is true of an individual also applies, more or less, to a people as a whole.

Mutual understanding would be immensely facilitated by the use of one universal tongue. But which shall it be, is the great question. At present it looks as if the English might be adopted as such, though it must be admitted that it is not the most suitable. Each language, of course, excels in some feature.... A practical answer to that momentous question must perforce be found in times to come, for it is manifest that by adopting one common language the onward march of man would be prodigiously quickened. I do not believe that an artificial concoction, like Volapuk, will ever find universal acceptance, however time-saving it might be. That would be contrary to human nature. Languages have grown into our hearts.

My brain is only a receiver. In the universe there is a core from which we obtain knowledge, strength, inspiration. I have not penetrated into the secrets of this core, but I know that it exists.

Of all things I liked books best. My father had a large library and whenever I could manage I tried to satisfy my passion for reading. He did not permit it and would fly in a rage when he caught me in the act. He hid the candles when he found that I was reading in secret. He did not want me to spoil my eyes. But I obtained tallow, made the wicking and cast the sticks into tin forms, and every night I would bush the keyhole and the cracks and read, often till dawn.

One day I went alone to the river to enjoy myself as usual. When I was a short distance from the masonry, however, I was horrified to observe that the water had risen and was carrying me along swiftly.... The pressure against my chest was great and I was barely able to keep my head above the surface.... Slowly and gradually I became exhausted and unable to withstand the strain longer. Just as I was about to let go, to be dashed against the rocks below, I saw in a flash of light a familiar diagram illustrating the hydraulic principle that the pressure of a fluid in motion is proportionate to the area exposed and automatically I turned on my left side. As if by magic, the pressure was reduced.

Our first endeavors are purely instinctive prompting of an imagination vivid and undisciplined. As we grow older reason asserts itself and we become more and more systematic and designing. But those early impulses, though not immediately productive, are of the greatest moment and may shape our very destinies. Indeed, I feel now that had I understood and cultivated instead of suppressing them, I would have added substantial value to my bequest to the world. But not until I had attained manhood did I realize that I was an inventor.

Our virtues and our failings are inseparable, like force and matter. When they separate, man is no more.

So we find that the three possible solutions of the great problem of increasing human energy are answered by the three words: food, peace, work. Many a year I have thought and pondered, lost myself in speculations and theories, considering man as a mass moved by a force, viewing his inexplicable movement in the light of a mechanical one, and applying the simple principles of mechanics to the analysis of the same until I arrived at these solutions, only to realize that they were taught to me in my early childhood. These three words sound the key-notes of the Christian religion. Their scientific meaning and purpose now clear to me: food to increase the mass, peace to diminish the retarding force, and work to increase the force accelerating human movement. These are the only three solutions which are possible of that great problem, and all of them have one object, one end, namely, to increase human energy. When we recognize this, we cannot help wondering how profoundly wise and scientific and how immensely practical the Christian religion is, and in what a marked contrast it stands in this respect to other religions. It is unmistakably the result of practical experiment and scientific observation which have extended through the ages, while other religions seem to be the outcome of merely abstract reasoning. Work, untiring effort, useful and accumulative, with periods of rest and recuperation aiming at higher efficiency, is its chief and ever-recurring command. Thus we are inspired both by Christianity and Science to do our utmost toward increasing the performance of mankind. This most important of human problems I shall now specifically consider.

I do not think you can name many great inventions that have been made by married men.

That electrical energy can be economically transmitted without wires to any terrestrial distance, I have unmistakably established in numerous observations, experiments and measurements, qualitative and quantitative. These have demonstrated that is practicable to distribute power from a central plant in unlimited amounts, with a loss not exceeding a small fraction of one per cent, in the transmission, even to the greatest distance, twelve thousand miles — to the opposite end of the globe.

The earth is bountiful, and where her bounty fails, nitrogen drawn from the air will refertilize her womb. I developed a process for this purpose in 1900. It was perfected fourteen years later under the stress of war by German chemists.

The distance at which it can strike, and the destructive power of such a quasi-intelligent machine being for all practical purposes unlimited, the gun, the armor of the battleship and the wall of the fortress, lose their import and significance. One can prophesy with a Daniel's confidence that skilled electricians will settle the battles of the near future. But this is the least. In its effect upon war and peace, electricity offers still much greater and more wonderful possibilities. To stop war by the perfection of engines of destruction alone, might consume centuries and centuries. Other means must be employed to hasten the end.

The harness of waterfalls is the most economical method known for drawing energy from the sun.

The history of science shows that theories are perishable. With every new truth that is revealed we get a better understanding of Nature and our conceptions and views are modified.

The human being is a self-propelled automaton entirely under the control of external influences. Willful and predetermined though they appear, his actions are governed not from within, but from without. He is like a float tossed about by the waves of a turbulent sea.

The ideal solution of the problem of transportation will be arrived at only when the complete annihilation of distance in the transmission of power in large amounts shall have become a commercial reality. That day we shall invade the domain of the bird. When the vexing problem of aerial navigation, which has defied his attempts for ages, is solved, man will advance with giant strides.

The individual is ephemeral, races and nations come and pass away, but man remains. Therein lies the profound difference between the individual and the whole.

Of the various branches of electrical investigation, perhaps the most interesting and immediately the most promising is that dealing with alternating currents.

All my money has been invested into experiments with which I have made new discoveries enabling mankind to have a little easier life.

The moment one constructs a device to carry into practice a crude idea, he finds himself unavoidably engrossed with the details of the apparatus. As he goes on improving and reconstructing, his force of concentration diminishes and he loses sight of the great underlying principle.... I do not rush into actual work. When I get an idea, I start at once building it up in my imagination. I change the construction, make improvements and operate the device in my mind. It is absolutely immaterial to me whether I run my turbine in thought or test it in my shop. I even note if it is out of balance.

The newspapers of the twenty-first century will give a mere 'stick' in the back pages to accounts of crime or political controversies, but will headline on the front pages the proclamation of a new scientific hypothesis.

The progressive development of man is vitally dependent on invention. It is the most important product of his creative brain. Its ultimate purpose is the complete mastery of mind over the material world, the harnessing of the forces of nature to human needs. This is the difficult task of the inventor who is often misunderstood and unrewarded. But he finds ample compensation in the pleasing exercises of his powers and in the knowledge of being one of that exceptionally privileged class without whom the race would have long ago perished in the bitter struggle against pitiless elements. Speaking for myself, I have already had more than my full measure of this exquisite enjoyment; so much, that for many years my life was little short of continuous rapture.

The scientists of today think deeply instead of clearly. One must be sane to think clearly, but one can think deeply and be quite insane.

The scientific man does not aim at an immediate result. He does not expect that his advanced ideas will be readily taken up. His work is like that of the planter — for the future. His duty is to lay the foundation for those who are to come, and point the way. He lives and labors and hopes.

The scientists from Franklin to Morse were clear thinkers and did not produce erroneous theories. The scientists of today think deeply instead of clearly. One must be sane to think clearly, but one can think deeply and be quite insane.

The Secretary of Hygiene or Physical Culture will be far more important in the cabinet of the President of the United States who holds office in the year 2035 than the Secretary of War.

The spread of civilization may be likened to a fire; first, a feeble spark, next a flickering flame, then a mighty blaze, ever increasing in speed and power.

The universal utilization of water power and its long-distance transmission will supply every household with cheap power and will dispense with the necessity of burning fuel. The struggle for existence being lessened, there should be development along ideal rather than material lines.

Archimedes was my ideal.

The year 2100 will see eugenics universally established. In past ages, the law governing the survival of the fittest roughly weeded out the less desirable strains. Then man's new sense of pity began to interfere with the ruthless workings of nature. As a result, we continue to keep alive and to breed the unfit.

There is no conflict between the ideal of religion and the ideal of science, but science is opposed to theological dogmas because science is founded on fact. To me, the universe is simply a great machine which never came into being and never will end. The human being is no exception to the natural order. Man, like the universe, is a machine. Nothing enters our minds or determines our actions which is not directly or indirectly a response to stimuli beating upon our sense organs from without. Owing to the similarity of our construction and the sameness of our environment, we respond in like manner to similar stimuli, and from the concordance of our reactions, understanding is barn. In the course of ages, mechanisms of infinite complexity are developed, but what we call "soul" or "spirit," is nothing more than the sum of the functioning of the body. When this functioning ceases, the "soul" or the "spirit" ceases likewise.

There is no memory or retentive faculty based on lasting impression. What we designate as memory is but increased responsiveness to repeated stimuli.

There is something within me that might be illusion as it is often case with young delighted people, but if I would be fortunate to achieve some of my ideals; it would be on the behalf of the whole of humanity. If those hopes would become fulfilled, the most exciting thought would be that it is a deed of a Serb.

Though free to think and act, we are held together, like the stars in the firmament, with ties inseparable. These ties cannot be seen, but we can feel them.

To conquer by sheer force is becoming harder and harder every day. Defensive is getting continuously the advantage of offensive, as we progress in the satanic science of destruction. The new art of controlling electrically the movements and operations of individualized automata at a distance without wires, will soon enable any country to render its coasts impregnable against all naval attacks.

To create and to annihilate material substance, cause it to aggregate in forms according to his desire, would be the supreme manifestation of the power of Man's mind, his most complete triumph over the physical world, his crowning achievement, which would place him beside his Creator, make him fulfill his Ultimate Destiny.

Today's scientists have substituted mathematics for experiments, and they wander off through equation after equation, and eventually build a structure which has no relation to reality.

In the twenty-first century, the robot will take the place which slave labor occupied in ancient civilization.

Universal Peace, assuming it to be in the fullest sense realizable, might not require eons for its accomplishment, however probable this may appear, judging from the imperceptibly slow growth of all great reformatory ideas of the past. ... Our accepted estimates of the duration of natural metamorphoses, or changes in general, have been thrown in doubt of late. The very foundations of science have been shaken.

We begin to think cosmically. Our sympathetic feelers reach out into the dim distance. The bacteria of the "Weltschmerz," are upon us. So far, however, universal harmony has been attained only in a single sphere of international relationship. That is the postal service. Its mechanism is working satisfactorily, but — how remote are we still from that scrupulous respect of the sanctity of the mail bag! And how much farther again is the next milestone on the road to peace — an international judicial service equally reliable as the postal!

We have soon to have everywhere smoke annihilators, dust absorbers, ozonizers, sterilizers of water, air, food and clothing, and accident preventers on streets, elevated roads and in subways. It will become next to impossible to contract disease germs or get hurt in the city, and country folk will got to town to rest and get well.

We wind a simple ring of iron with coils; we establish the connections to the generator, and with wonder and delight we note the effects of strange forces which we bring into play, which allow us to transform, to transmit and direct energy at will.

Whatever the future may bring, the universal application of these great principles is fully assured, though it may be long in coming. With the opening of the first power plant, incredulity will give way to wonderment, and this to ingratitude, as ever before.

When a coil is operated with currents of very high frequency, beautiful brush effects may be produced, even if the coil be of comparatively small dimensions. The experimenter may vary them in many ways, and, if it were nothing else, they afford a pleasing sight.

When we speak of man, we have a conception of humanity as a whole, and before applying scientific methods to the investigation of his movement we must accept this as a physical fact.

While I am not a believer in the orthodox sense, I commend religion, first, because every individual should have some ideal — religious, artistic, scientific, or humanitarian — to give significance to his life. Second, because all the great religions contain wise prescriptions relating to the conduct of life, which hold good now as they did when they were promulgated.

With ideas it is like with dizzy heights you climb:
At first they cause you discomfort and you are
anxious to get down, distrustful of your own
powers; but soon the remoteness of the turmoil of
life and the inspiring influence of the altitude calm
your blood; your step gets firm and sure and you
begin to look - for dizzier heights.

Made in the USA
Middletown, DE
16 February 2020

84890709R00050